I S👓e Insects

Dragonfly

written by **August Hoeft**

xist Publishing

INSPIRING DISCOVERY & DELIGHT

2

I see a dragonfly.

The dragonfly is blue.

The dragonfly has four wings.

The dragonfly eats insects.

The dragonfly lives near water.

I see a
dragonfly.

12

Things to do next!

Write a Sentence

I see a _____.

Drawing

Make a drawing of your favorite insect.

Sharing

Talk to your classmates about your favorite picture in this book. Explain to them why you like it.

WORD LIST

a	is
blue	lives
dragonfly	near
eats	see
four	the
has	water
I	wings
insects	

Dragonfly
ISBN: 978-1-5324-2858-6 PB

9 781532 428586   90000

August Hoeft

I S👓e Insects
Bee

August Hoeft

xist Publishing

A Note to Parents & Teachers—

Welcome to I See Insects from Xist Publishing! These books are designed to inspire discovery and delight in the youngest readers. Each book features very simple sentences with visual cues to help beginners read their very first text.

You can help each child develop a lifetime love of reading right from the very start. Here are some ways to help a beginning reader get going:

 Read the book aloud as a first introduction

 Run your fingers below the words as you read each line

 Give the child the chance to finish the sentences or read repeating words while you read the rest.

 Encourage the child to read aloud every day!

Published proudly in the State of Texas, USA by Xist Publishing
www.xistpublishing.com
24200 Southwest Freeway Suite 402- 290 Rosenberg, TX 77471
All images licensed from Adobe Stock
First Edition

Saddle Stitch ISBN: 978-1-5324-2854-8
Perfect Bound ISBN: 978-1-5324-4152-3
Hardcover: 978-1-5324-3337-5
eISBN: 978-1-5324-2829-6